Volume Eight

HABITAT

Volume Eight

HABITAT

Curtis J. Badger

STACKPOLE BOOKS

Published by
STACKPOLE BOOKS
Cameron and Kelker Streets
P.O. Box 1831
Harrisburg, PA 17105

Printed in the United States of America

10 9 8 7 6 5 4 3 2

First edition

*Cover design by Tracy Patterson with
Mark Olszewski*

Interior design by Marcia Lee Dobbs

Library of Congress Cataloging-in-Publication Data
(Revised for volume 8)

Badger, Curtis J.
    Bird Carving basics.

    Contents: v. 1. Eyes — v. 2. Feet —
v. 7. Special painting techniques — v. 8. Habitat.
    1. Wood-carving. 2. Birds in art. I. Title.
TT199.7.B33   1990   731.4'62   90–9491
ISBN 0–8117–2334–8 (v. 1)

Contents

Acknowledgments

Many thanks to Charlie Berry, Jo Craemer, Larry Tawes, Jr., and Rich Smoker. This book would not have been possible without the generous cooperation of these artists. They not only allowed me to look over their shoulders as they worked, but in many cases they took the time to create special projects especially for this volume.

Wildfowl art seems to be a sharing process, and it's not coincidental that many of our best artists are also talented teachers. All full-time, professional wildlife artists were at one time beginners who depended on a more experienced friend to teach them the technical aspects of the art. And, of course, the best artists never stop learning—they are always trying new techniques, new methods of expression. The sharing of information has thus played a major role in the growing popularity of bird carving and other venues of wildfowl art.

So to Charlie, Jo, Larry, and Rich: Many thanks for keeping the tradition alive. Thanks for sharing.

Introduction

If your interest in wildfowl art begins and ends with hunting-style decoys, this might not be the book for you. But if you want to create decorative works that go far beyond the basic rendering of a wooden bird, then I think we have some special treats for you in these pages.

Too often wildfowl artists concentrate so completely on the accurate rendering of a bird that they fall flat when the time comes to create a setting in which to place the bird. As a result, the overall quality of the work suffers.

Creating habitat should never be an afterthought. A decorative carving that includes a bird or birds presented in a setting is considered by the viewer a single piece of sculpture. The birds and their habitat must function as a whole. The habitat should complement and enhance the carving of the bird, never detract from it or overpower it.

In creating contemporary decorative pieces, artists must not only have superior technical skills in bird carving, but they must also be creative and skillful in selecting and constructing the proper habitat.

That's what this book is about. If you need to create leaves, grass, ice, snow, water, mushrooms, or even assorted insects and reptiles to accompany your bird carving, we'll show you how. And we hope to spark your imagination. Perhaps one of the sessions shown here will encourage you to develop your own techniques, to find a special way of creating habitat that's yours alone.

One of the enjoyable aspects of making habitat is discovering new uses for everyday objects. Jo Craemer dismantles a metal pot scrubber and uses the pieces to create moss. A jalapeño pepper from her garden, she discovers, makes a great mold for shaping mushroom caps. Larry Tawes, Jr., uses thin brass shim stock to create cordgrass for a marsh scene. Rich Smoker rolls out a bead of plumber's putty, drapes it over a tree limb, and creates a garter snake.

Although we'll discuss the use of epoxies, metal, paper, wire, and other materials, the most traditional source of habitat material is, of course, good old-fashioned wood. Although carvers are very creative when it comes to applying synthetic materials to their art, wood has a special quality, a purity that other materials lack. Indeed, some wildfowl art competitions require that the pieces entered be made almost exclusively of wood.

Whether to carve your mushroom caps from tupelo or to mold them with epoxy putty is a personal and professional decision. It's up to you. In this book, we'll show you creative ways of making habitat from wood, epoxy, and various other materials. You have the luxury of picking and choosing the techniques that are right for you.

The materials used here come from a variety of sources. Most carving-supply dealers sell metal, paper, and synthetic products intended for creating a variety of habitat. Contemporary carvers like to explore hardware stores and plumbing-supply outlets, because very often tools and materials lend themselves to carving projects. And don't forget the taxidermy-supply houses. They offer goods and gadgets that can fill a particular need for bird carvers.

Often the key to solving a particular habitat dilemma is where you least expect to find it, as when Jo Craemer found the perfect mold for mushroom caps growing in her garden. But that's what makes bird carving—and especially the creation of habitat—a challenging and fulfilling task.

1 Charlie Berry
Creating a Cornfield

At age seventy-seven, Charlie Berry still has the look of an athlete and coach—a compact build, a springy step, a salt-and-pepper crewcut, and a gravelly voice that can still reach out and touch a lineman who might be giving less than his all.

For more than thirty years Charlie was a teacher, coach, and supervisor in Maryland's Wicomico County school system, a job that gave him a role in sculpting thousands of young lives. Today he is a bird sculptor of the first rank.

Charlie specializes in miniature carvings of waterfowl, and in this session he demonstrates his technique for creating a cornfield. The field will be a setting for a Canada goose he is working on, but it could be used with a wide variety of wildfowl. He carves each ear of corn by rounding a piece of basswood with a knife, cutting little flaps of wood around the circumference to suggest the shuck, then using a burning pen to etch each individual kernel. A one-eighth-inch dowel will be the cornstalk, and leaves will be made from thin copper.

"I got interested in carving when I quit hunting in the early sixties," he tells me. "I grew up in New Castle, Delaware, which was pretty rural at that time, and I hunted ducks and geese all my life. But it got so in the sixties you couldn't walk out the door without breaking a law, and that took all the fun out of it. Dan Brown (another Salisbury-area carver who has lent his expertise to this series) played football for me at Wicomico High in the forties and he got me started. So somewhere around 1963 I went from hunting birds to carving them."

When he retired in 1975 Charlie immediately launched his second full-time career as a bird carver. "My problem was that I couldn't paint very well," he says. "But I kept working at it and gradually improved. When the Ward Foundation held its first competition I won four or five blue ribbons, but the carvings were terrible compared to what's being done today."

But Charlie's carvings improved along with those of other artists, and he later won a best-in-show in miniatures with a preening black duck. He no longer enters the competition, but for the past twenty years he has been a regular at the Ward fall exhibition and

Charlie begins the project by coating a wooden base with yellow carpenter's glue, then applying dry, sandy soil while the glue is still wet. Charlie uses a kitchen strainer to sift the soil, removing organic material and other debris. You can use beach sand, Charlie says, but he prefers the darker sandy loam of his backyard garden. The soil will dry to a slightly darker value when it is glued to the base.

Charlie applies one coat, allows it to dry, removes excess particles, then applies a second coat. When applying the second coat, he will often thicken the soil in some areas, creating small furrows if he is making a farm field.

has served on the Ward Foundation Board of Trustees. He attends six or seven national bird art exhibitions each year, which give him and his wife a chance to visit friends and see the country. They have toured all but two of the fifty states.

Charlie's two careers have each brought their rewards. His jewellike miniature carvings are eagerly sought by collectors, and the dividends of his career in education continue to grow. The other day a former student, now a successful businessman in the Midwest, stopped by to say hello. He hadn't seen his old teacher and coach for decades, but he was in Salisbury and wanted to pay a visit and to say thanks.

"I didn't get paid extra for coaching," Charlie says, "and back then I could have used the money. But the real rewards are seeing your students become successful, taking pride in their accomplishments. To me, that's more valuable than any amount of money."

The ears of corn are made of basswood, and here Charlie uses a knife to round a section of wood. Habitat such as corn should be in correct proportion to the size of the bird that will be used in the carving. Charlie plans to use a four-inch Canada goose with this arrangement, so the ears of corn will be about one inch long.

First Charlie creates an open husk at the end of the ear by using a small, sharp knife to peel away thin layers of wood.

3

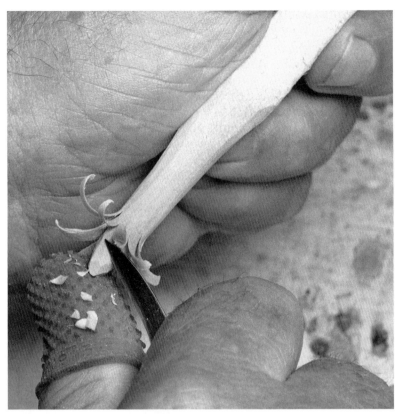

After peeling away the layers, Charlie uses the small knife to carve the ear. The end of the ear should be slightly rounded.

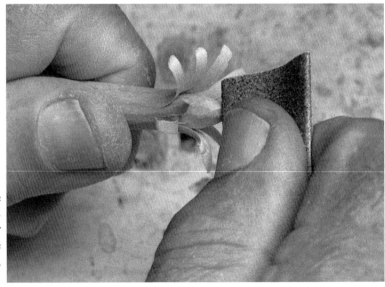

Before burning the individual kernels of corn, sandpaper is used to remove knife marks from the ear.

4

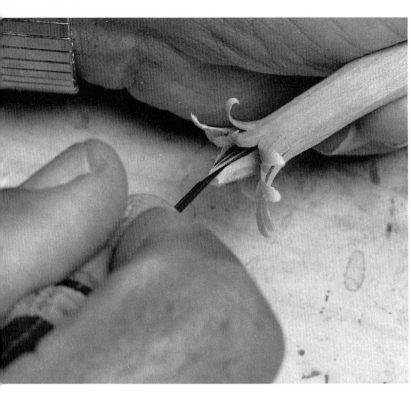

The burning pen has a sharp blade that can be heated to a variable range of temperatures. To burn the kernels, Charlie turns the thermostat up so the blade will slightly scorch the wood. The dark lines will provide depth and definition when the kernels are painted.

Charlie begins by burning lines along the length of the ear, then burns across the ear to create a cross-hatch pattern. Burning the ear is easier with the corn husk pulled back. After burning, he will glue the layers partially closed, covering the portion of the ear not reached with the pen tip.

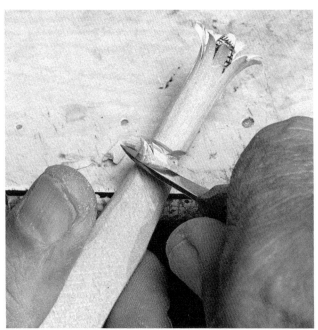

With the kernel carved and the husk glued partially closed, Charlie cuts a notch and removes the ear from the length of basswood.

He rounds off the base of the ear. The rough point on the base will remain; it resembles the stem of a real ear of corn. Sandpaper will be used to remove the knife marks.

Final detail is added to the outside of the husk with the burning pen. Charlie burns shallow lines along the length of the ear to depict the overlapping of the husk.

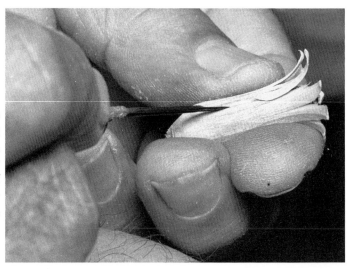

Cornstalks are made from one-eighth-inch wooden dowels. The field Charlie is creating has already been harvested, so most of the stalks will be broken, and some will appear only as short nubs emerging from the ground. He is cutting this one somewhat longer and will mount the ear of corn he just carved on the stalk.

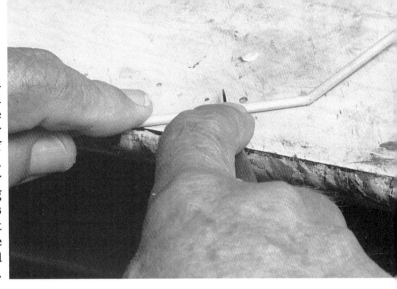

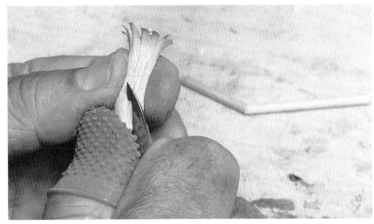

Charlie cuts a shallow notch in the base of the ear where it will attach to the stalk.

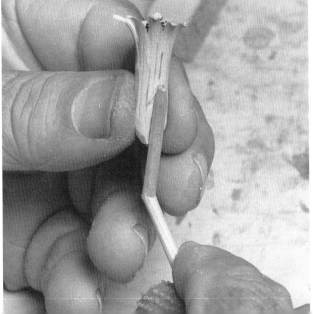

A small dab of Super Glue, Duco cement, or a similar adhesive is used to attach the ear to the stalk.

A drill fitted with a one-eighth-inch bit (to accommodate the one-eighth-inch wooden dowels used to create the cornstalks) applies holes in the base. Charlie drills the holes at an angle of about 60 to 75 degrees, because the stalks will have been pushed over by harvesting equipment.

The angles at which the holes are drilled should be varied slightly so they will not appear too uniform. The stalks should all be leaning in the same direction.

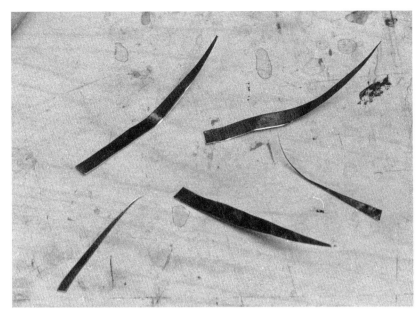

Thin copper strips are cut with scissors to the approximate shape of corn leaves. Some of these will be glued to stalks; others will be placed on the ground.

The stalk with the ear of corn and leaf attached is planted in the cornfield.

The cornfield makes a perfect setting for a Canada goose. A few loose ears of corn and some copper leaves have been added. Charlie's final step will be to paint the leaves and add them to the stalks.

The finished carving, enhanced by habitat.

2

Jo Craemer
Creating Moss with a Brillo Pad

"In creating any habitat, one of my major concerns is durability and the ability of the habitat to withstand cleaning and dusting over the years," says Jo Craemer.

Various items can be used to create moss, but most of them are very fragile or will deteriorate in time, which is not exactly a good selling point for an expensive carving. Jo uses a common kitchen pot scrubber called Brillo, which is made of tightly meshed copper. Similar products under other brand names are also available. Try a little experimentation to find the texture and material best suited for your work.

In this session, Jo makes a few mossy sprigs to place around the base of a tree trunk. The Brillo can be left in its original dense configuration, or it can be pulled apart into strings that, when properly painted, resemble Spanish moss.

Jo is a retired Navy nurse who lives near Georgetown, Delaware. Jo began carving after attending the Mid-Atlantic Wildfowl Carving Exhibition while stationed in Virginia Beach, Virginia, in the early 1980s. She signed up for a course with world champion artist Lynn Forehand of Chesapeake, and from then on she was hooked on bird carving.

In recent years she has returned to the Mid-Atlantic as a competitor and has taken home a number of ribbons. In 1988 she entered the prestigious Ward Competition for the first time and won an honorable mention. Her goal now is to continue her rapid improvement and to compete at the top level of the art.

Jo credits her rapid rise to courses she has taken with such talented carvers as Forehand, Larry Barth, Bob Guge, Ernie Muehlmatt, and Greg Woodard. "Starting out with Lynn Forehand cut five years out of the learning process," she says. "I didn't have any bad habits. I didn't have any habits at all. What I learned from him in a few days would have taken me months or years on my own. Studying with these master carvers has accelerated the learning curve tremendously. Now I'm concentrating on developing my own style, which comes with experience."

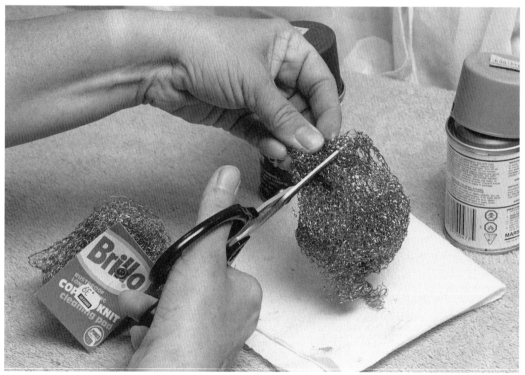

Jo begins by clipping off a bit of the scrub pad with scissors. She advises using copper rather than stainless steel pads because they hold a shape better and can be briefly heated if necessary. The pads are available in fine and coarse textures, so pick the type best suited to the piece you are working on, or combine the textures.

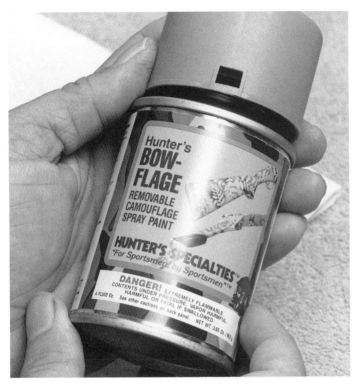

The copper pads can be primed and painted with spray paint. Jo uses a camouflage spray designed for use on bows and guns, which serves as both the primer and the finish coat. The camo paint, she says, dries flat and is available in a variety of natural colors.

A large clip holds the sprig of Brillo while Jo applies the paint. With this gadget she can turn the Brillo to any angle and cover all the copper without camouflaging her left hand. Several thin coats look better than one heavy one, she advises.

A heavy handful of moss has been painted and is ready to be applied to a carving. Camouflage paints such as the one shown here are available in most sporting goods stores or in the hunting and archery sections of department stores. If you can't find camo paint, any flat-drying spray paint of the proper color will do.

Brillo at work. Through the magic of camouflage paint, a pot scrubber is disguised as a realistic bit of Spanish moss. The mushrooms on the right are closely related to jalapeño peppers, as our next session will illustrate.

3

Jo Craemer
Peppers and Mushrooms (Hold the Pizza)

This technique for making mushrooms was one of Jo's "2:00 A.M. brainstorms," the product of a sleepless night, unfinished carvings, and a big exhibition near at hand. It's one of those simple techniques that takes someone with a fertile imagination—and a need for quick mushrooms—to come up with.

Jo uses jalapeño peppers from her garden as molds for making mushroom caps with two-part epoxy. She simply mixes the epoxy, coaxes it over the cap of a suitably shaped pepper, removes it when it hardens, then fills it with more epoxy and makes an epoxy stem. Detailing and painting complete the process.

"For carvings you plan to enter in competition, it's best to make as much habitat as you can from wood," she says. "But when it's not important to you to make everything from wood, interesting habitat can be made from a variety of materials, and your imagination is the only limit."

Jo uses two-part epoxy available at plumbing-supply and hardware stores. This material is called "propoxy 20" and is steel reinforced, so don't let anyone try to add your mushrooms to his pizza topping. Jo uses a knife to slice off a section of the material, which incorporates both the epoxy resin and the catalyst.

15

The material is worked by hand until the light and dark colors are blended into a uniform gray.

The epoxy is then smoothed over the head of a small jalapeño pepper.
The pepper makes a good mold because its surface is slightly flexible and waxy, so the epoxy is easy to remove after it has hardened.

After spreading the epoxy over the top of the pepper, Jo moistens her finger with alcohol and smooths the surface of the mushroom cap.

While the cap is hardening, she will use leftover epoxy to roll out little mushroom stems. Each stem is bent slightly.

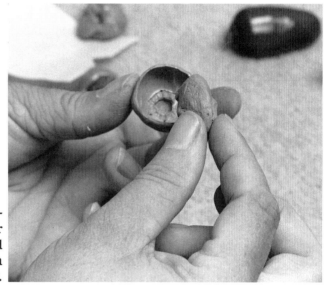

The hardened cap is removed from the pepper and soft epoxy is pressed into the hardened mushroom cap, filling it completely.

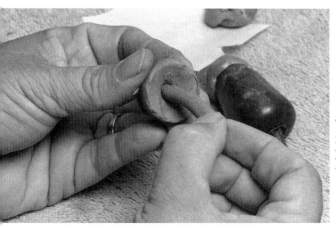

Then one of the gently bent mushroom stems, which by now has hardened sufficiently, is attached to the cap of the mushroom.

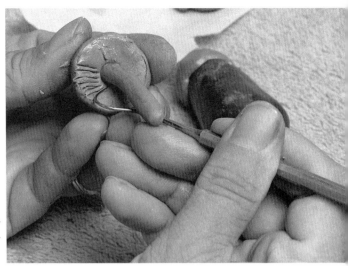

Jo uses a dental tool to emboss little gills under the cap of the mushroom. A piece of stiff wire could be used instead.

She applies acrylic paint to the mushrooms with an airbrush, using a mushroom field guide to determine color and shading. The airbrush gives a nice, soft effect, but a brush could be used. She finishes each mushroom with five or six thin washes of matte medium, which provides a leathery look.

Jo's jalapeño mushrooms look like the real thing. (The mushrooms shown at the end of chapter 2, cemented to the base of a carving, were made with different size peppers as molds and were painted a light brown. Colors can range from brown to tan to gold, or even red.)

4

Jo Craemer
Making Grass from Copper Sheets

Jo says she learned this very efficient technique for making rolls of copper grass from a fellow student at the Ward Foundation's Summer Carving Seminar in Salisbury, Maryland. Instead of cutting and detailing one blade at a time, with this technique you make an entire clump of grass at once, which speeds up the procedure significantly.

Although in this session Jo makes the grass before painting it, the procedure could be streamlined even more by painting the copper sheets before cutting out and detailing the blades of grass. Before painting, degrease the copper sheets with acetone, then apply a bare metal primer. Some primer colors resemble dead grass and can be used as the final coat. Jo usually uses hunter's camouflage paint, which comes in flat-drying natural colors, or Jo Sonya acrylic paints applied with either a brush or an airbrush. She uses a slightly lighter color value on the back side of each blade for a natural look.

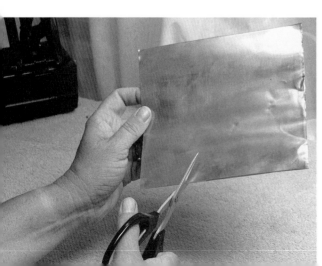

Jo begins by cutting a sheet of copper at a diagonal as shown. This will provide both long and short blades of grass. The steeper the angle, the more difference there will be in blade length. The .005-inch copper sheets are available at most carving-supply dealers.

The grass blades should be lightly sketched on the copper sheet with a pencil. The heavy markings in this photograph were made for illustration purposes only. Jo usually draws only the center line of each blade. It is easier to shape the clump if a small gap is left between each blade.

Jo cuts out each blade of copper, leaving an uncut band along the bottom connecting the blades.

Individual blades of grass have one or more center veins, depending upon the variety. Jo places the copper on a soft surface and uses a putty knife (or a similar instrument) to emboss the center vein in each blade. In this photo, she has embossed only the shorter blades on the left, which will be removed in the next step.

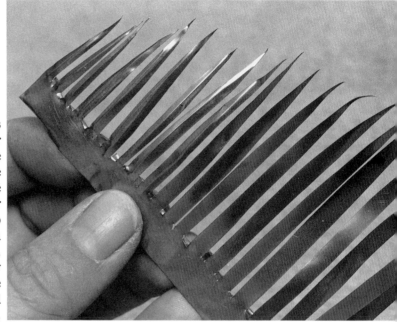

The clump will be made with the shorter blades, so Jo uses the scissors to remove them from the band. Several smaller clumps of grass look more natural than one large one, she says. Jo advises caution when handling thin sheets of copper because the edges are very sharp.

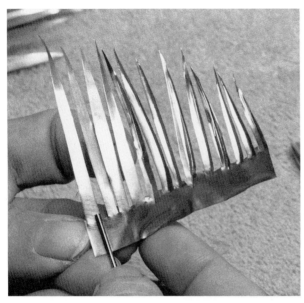

A piece of wire or small piece of metal is handy for beginning the rolled clump of grass. Here Jo begins rolling the copper band around a small drill bit, starting with the taller blades.

The copper band of grass is tightly rolled around the drill bit. Because Jo started with the taller blades, they will be on the inside of the clump, where they should be.

Once the band has been rolled tightly, Jo separates and shapes the blades, creating a pleasing composition.

Two different sizes of clumps, made from the same wedge of copper.

These copper blades of grass were used on Jo's carving of a Baltimore oriole.

The copper clumps are incorporated into the base of a carving. If the base has already been made, simply drill a hole of the proper diameter and glue the clumps in place.

5
Making Paper Grass

Jo Craemer

While copper grass is sturdy and practically indestructible, paper grass is easier to make and more realistic looking. The only drawback is the relatively fragile nature of paper, but then again no one is planning on having a hockey match using your carving as the puck. As a general rule, if you want long, graceful blades of grass, use copper. For short grass and small leaves, paper will do a fine job.

Jo says she learned the technique she demonstrates in this session from world champion carver Ernie Muehlmatt of Pennsylvania, whom she describes as a genius at making realistic leaves and grass. Basically, she paints a sheet of paper with acrylic paints, cuts out blades of grass, dampens them with water, then uses a burning pen to emboss detail and add a realistic curve to each blade.

"I've used all sorts of brown paper for making grass," says Jo. "Grocery bags and shopping bags are fairly heavy, and they will work well. But I prefer a special paper I buy from Birds of a Feather [24 Dewey St., Sayville, NY 11782, 516-589-0707]. Their 'leaf paper' is thin and flexible and seems to be denser than paper bags."

For the sake of efficiency, Jo paints the paper before cutting out blades of grass. "Even if you plan to use brown paper to simulate dead grass, I recommend painting both sides of the paper with acrylic paint to seal it and to prevent the grass from later losing its shape if it is exposed to a hot, humid environment," she says. "I've found that painting one side of the paper with a slightly darker color makes the finished grass more realistic looking. I don't try for an even coat of paint. Leaving a few streaks and color variations looks natural on the finished grass. If for some reason you don't want to paint the sheet before cutting out the grass, you could cut out the blades and then dip them into small containers of paint."

Jo makes copper grass in rolls or clumps, but she makes paper grass one blade at a time. "The copper can be shaped after being cut out," she says, "but the paper blades assume a permanent shape from the burning tool. If you tried to cut out a band of blades like you do with copper, you'd end up with an unruly mess."

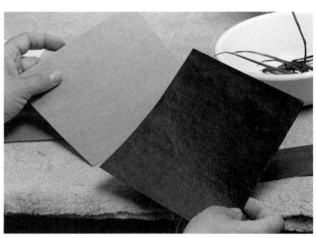

Jo coats both sides of the paper with Liquitex acrylic paint to seal the surface and provide the proper color for the project she's working on. The sheet on the right has been painted dark green, and the one on the left is brown, just right for creating a fall or winter setting.

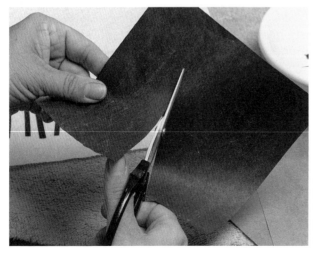

As in the procedure for making copper grass, Jo cuts the sheet at a diagonal so it will be easy to make blades of various lengths.

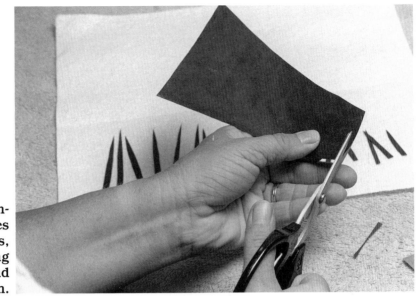

Jo cuts out individual blades of grass, slightly varying the length and width of each.

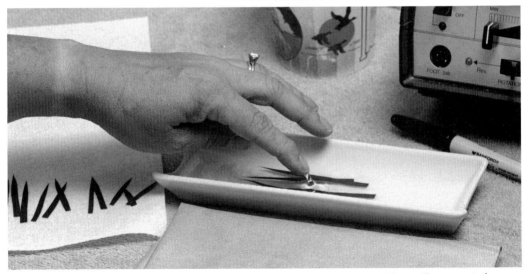

A little water is added to a shallow, flat container. (This happens to be a dish designed for serving corn on the cob.) Individual blades are dipped into the water for just a few seconds. "The paper should be damp, not wet," Jo says. "Don't let it soak in the water." After being dampened, the paper blade is blotted on a paper towel to remove excess moisture.

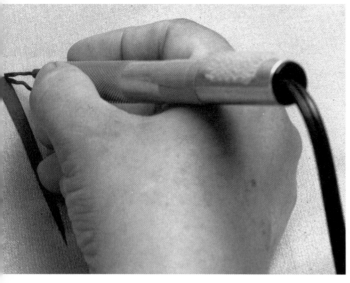

Jo places the blade on a soft surface—she uses a section of an old ironing board cover—and prepares to "iron" on detail with the burning pen. The tip of the pen should not be sharp; you want it to emboss a crease in the paper, not cut through it. "Use enough heat to press in the veins of the grass, but not enough to burn the paper," says Jo. "You should hear the damp paper hiss slightly as you pull the pen down the blade of grass. Pull the pen slowly enough to dry the paper as you go."

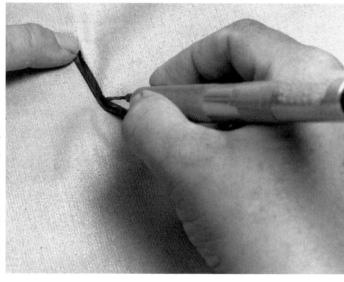

Jo holds the blade of grass with her finger while slowly pulling the tip of the burning pen from the base to the end of the blade. Holding the paper flat while burning produces a fairly straight blade of grass.

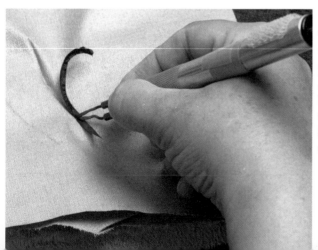

To get a curlier blade, Jo applies the burning pen without holding the paper down. To produce a spiral, Jo begins creasing one side of the blade, then turns it over and creases the other side. Use your imagination and don't be afraid to experiment, she advises.

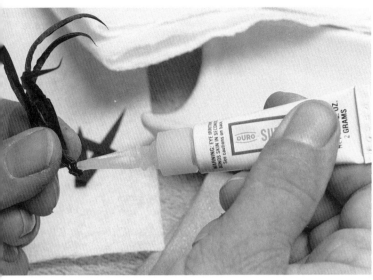

Jo gathers an assortment of different lengths and shapes of grass blades, twists the paper together at the base, then saturates the base with Super Glue.

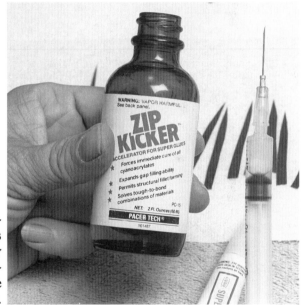

Zip Kicker is a chemical accelerator for Super Glue; it makes the glue harden instantly. Only one drop is needed, and Jo applies the solution with a syringe that has a blunted needle.

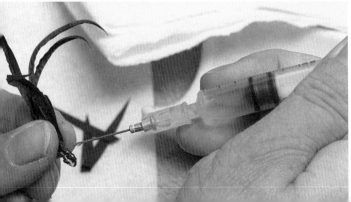

With the syringe filled with Zip Kicker, the warmth of Jo's hand is sufficient to make the chemical expand slightly, forcing out a drop. The Super Glue cures almost instantly when the accelerator makes contact with it.

With the glue hardened, Jo arranges the blades of grass in the shape she wants. This clump is made up of long, graceful blades curving in the same direction.

This clump is made of five shorter individual blades.

The same technique can be used for creating leaves of evergreen trees, like this little spruce bough that is part of a Baltimore oriole habitat.

6
Making Paper Leaves

Jo Craemer

Extremely realistic leaves can be made from paper. A little heavy paper, some natural color acrylic paints, and a burning pen can produce exceptional fall leaves that are nicely wrinkled and mottled. The burning pen has a sharp, heated tip and is similar in design to a soldering iron. It is commonly used in wood carving and pyrographic art, and most contemporary bird carvers have at least one in their arsenal of tools. The pen is used to burn in feather barbs, quills, and other fine detail where the combination of heat and a sharp edge creates a very fine, clean line.

Jo uses the burning pen on dampened paper to add fine detail to grass and leaves. She uses a fairly blunt blade to avoid cutting the paper and just enough heat to emboss detail such as veins in leaves and grass. When making fall leaves with paper, the burning pen can create scorch marks that add to the weathered look of a leaf.

Because paper leaves are fairly fragile, Jo usually uses them in areas where they will not be handled. Fall leaves, made of paper, can be scattered on the ground of a particular habitat. For leaves that will be attached to branches, she uses copper or brass.

Jo begins the leaf-making process just as she did when making paper grass in chapter 5. Heavy paper is coated on both sides with Liquitex acrylic paint in whatever color is appropriate for the habitat under construction. Mottled, streaked paint is more realistic than a uniform color, so just this once allow yourself to be sloppy.

Jo keeps a comprehensive reference file of habitat items. She photocopies real leaves, fronds, and similar items, then uses the photocopy as a template when tracing the outline of a leaf on painted paper.

A copy machine is handy for making reference material. These sheets were created by placing various leaves in the copier. This material comes in handy when it's February, the trees are bare, and a handful of oak leaves are badly needed for a carving project. If you don't have access to a copier, you can place a sheet of white paper over a leaf, then rub gently with a soft lead pencil. The rubbing will yield a surprising amount of detail.

Jo traces the outline of a leaf onto paper that has been painted with Liquitex acrylic.

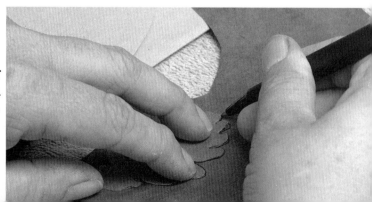

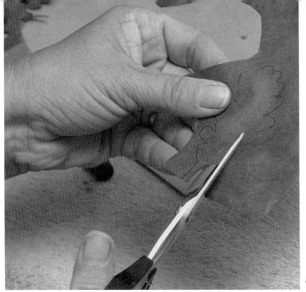

The leaf is cut out with scissors.

Jo compares the shape of the paper leaf (right) with the real thing.

The paper leaf is dipped in water for a few seconds to dampen it. Then the burning pen is used to emboss veins and other detail. Jo frequently refers to the real leaf to ensure accuracy. She uses a soft surface on which to do the burning, because the pen tip must press into the paper fibers slightly.

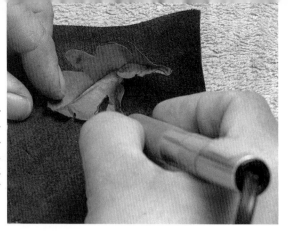

The tip of the burning pen should be dull and just hot enough to dry the moisture as it is pulled along the paper. The paper leaf will twist and curl realistically as it is dried with the burning pen. Try burning first on one side of the leaf, then the other.

When creating weathered leaves for a fall or winter habitat, Jo cranks up the heat and singes the edges slightly and burns small leaf-mold holes.

A variety of leaves. From left: a real leaf, a paper cutout, and two detailed paper leaves. Jo makes realistic stems for her paper leaves by twisting the paper stems into a tight cylinder, then dipping them in Elmer's wood glue.

7

Jo Craemer
Decking the Halls with Copper Holly

In this session Jo will make holly leaves from copper sheeting, holly berries from two-part epoxy, and holly branches from heavy copper wire. The techniques are very similar to those used in making paper leaves. A leaf outline is traced onto copper and cut out, then textured not with a burning pen but with a blade and a burnishing tool. A wire stem is attached to the leaf, which in turn is attached to a copper branch. Epoxy is rolled into little berry balls, which are attached to the branches with wire. A final coating of epoxy bark covers the stems and branches, then the piece is primed and painted.

The branches in this demonstration were made from thick copper wire salvaged from Jo's local electric company. The heaviest wire was used as grounding cable on power poles, and it was discarded when the company installed a new pole. A thoughtful neighborhood electrical contractor supplied other bits and pieces, which were left over from a construction project.

The basic form of the branch is created by soldering progressively smaller gauges of wire onto the heaviest "limb." Jo uses a real holly branch, or a suitable photograph of one, as a model when creating her own metal and epoxy version.

As she did when making a paper leaf in chapter 6, Jo begins by tracing the outline of a real leaf onto a thin sheet of copper. This .005-inch material is available through most carving suppliers.

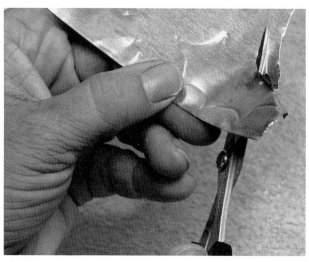

The copper leaf is then cut out with scissors. The edges of the metal are very sharp, so handle the copper leaves carefully. Jo leaves a fairly wide stem on the leaf; it will later be wrapped around a wire and attached to a branch.

Jo cuts out several leaves at a time. Those not used in the current project will be kept for future use.

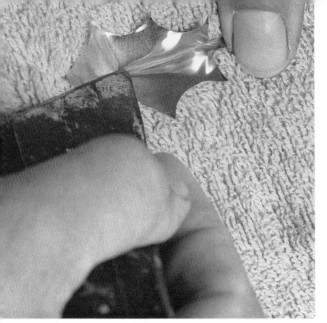

Once the veins are pressed in, Jo uses a burnishing tool to flatten and shape the copper between the veins, working on the opposite side of the leaf.

The vein can be pressed into the leaf with most any fairly sharp tool. Jo uses a putty knife here. A real leaf is used as reference in determining the configuration of veins.

The copper should be worked on a soft, pliable surface so that it will "bend" slightly under the embossing tools. Jo uses a piece of soft leather.

With the veins installed and the areas between them shaped with the burnishing tool, the leaf begins to curl realistically.

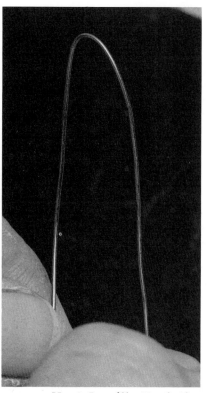

Jo uses needle-nose pliers to get a tight twist. Two smaller pieces of wire twisted together are stronger than one larger piece, she says.

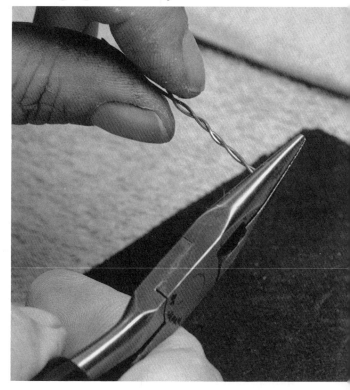

Next Jo will attach the stem, which is made with a piece of small wire bent in half and twisted together.

The pliers are used to crimp the copper stem of the leaf around the twisted wire.

At this step we see the importance of leaving the wide copper stem when cutting out the leaf early in this session. The copper wraps around the wire, holding it in place until the joint can be strengthened with Super Glue.

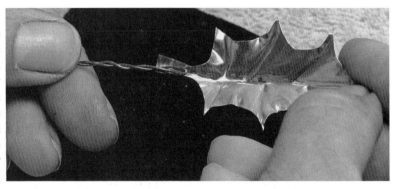

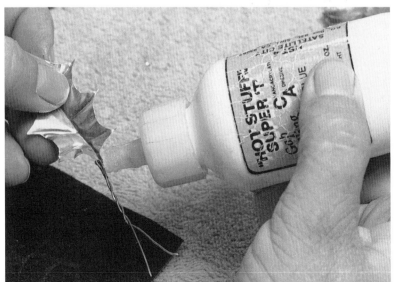

Jo applies a few drops of Super Glue, then adds Zip Kicker, an accelerator that causes the glue to cure very quickly. (For instructions on applying Zip Kicker see chapter 5.)

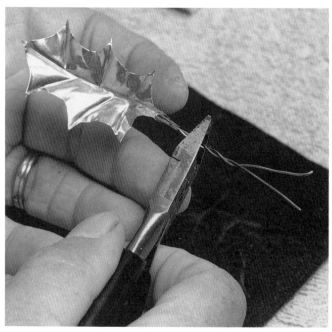

When the glue hardens,
the stem is clipped off with
wire cutters.

Jo makes her branches with a variety of materials,
including hollow brass rods and copper wire. The
heavy-gauge ground wire, salvaged from the local
electric utility, is used for the main branch. Jo
notches the larger wire, then attaches with solder
smaller-gauge wire to create smaller branches.

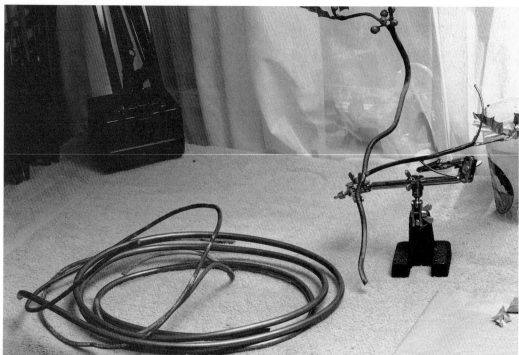

This close-up shows a solder joint. Although Jo uses solder to create the main branch, she will use Super Glue to attach the leaves and stems and the holly berries. "I have never been able to figure out how to solder a group of leaves without having the solder in previously attached leaves melt as I do succeeding ones," she says. "I end up with everything falling apart. Soldering does make a neater and stronger joint, though. So if you can do it . . ."

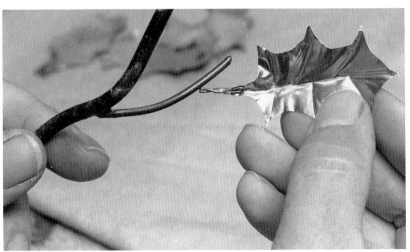

Instead, Jo will attach the leaves with Super Glue assisted by the Zip Kicker accelerator. An advantage of using a thick glue is that it will help fill gaps.

Super Glue has been applied to the leaf, and now Zip Kicker is added, creating an instant bond. Although the glue joint is not as strong as solder, a later application of epoxy "bark" will further strengthen the joints.

The holly berries are made of two-part epoxy available in plumbing supply and hardware stores. The material she is using here was also used to make the mushrooms in chapter 3.

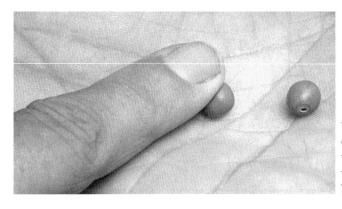

The two parts of the epoxy are mixed by hand until they produce a uniform color, then round berries are rolled out.

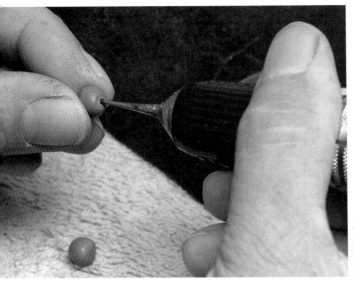

A high-speed grinder with
a drill bit is used to put a hole
in each berry, where a wire
stem will be attached.

A single strand of
wire is pressed into
the hole, creating the
stem. Berries can be
created with a
variety of synthetic
materials, or they can
be carved from wood.

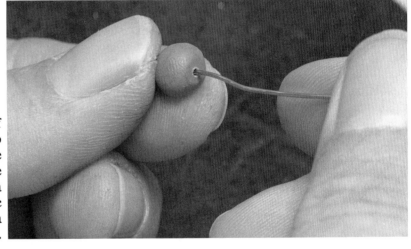

With the branches
and leaves attached, Jo
is ready to put on
some berries. They will
be attached with
Super Glue and Zip
Kicker in the same man-
ner as the leaves.

The branch is finished by applying an epoxy bark, which helps strengthen the piece. A medium such as Liquitex Modeling Paste can be used, but Jo prefers the more pliable qualities of epoxy, which allow the wire branches to be bent later if need be. She brushes on an epoxy paste called PC–7, which is available at most hardware stores. When the epoxy dries, Jo cleans the branch with alcohol or acetone, sprays with bare metal primer, then paints with Jo Sonya acrylics. The berries are first painted white, then red. The white base coat intensifies the transparent washes of red that cover it. If the leaves and berries look too flat after painting, some gloss can be added with a wash or two of matte medium and a discreet touch of gloss medium.

Some examples of other copper leaves shaped by a putty knife and burnishing tool.

8

Jo Craemer
Of Snow and Ice and Sleet and Rain

"I've seen a lot of carvings at competitions displayed on beautiful snow-covered habitat," says Jo. "While I admired the beauty, I wondered how the snow would fare over the years as dust and dirt accumulated. I wanted to find a way to make snow that would look light and fluffy, yet withstand years of cleaning and dusting and remain as white as the day I made it."

Jo's experiments yielded several methods. Her favorite is a fairly simple procedure involving a two-part plastic material called EnviroTex (available at art and craft stores), loose cotton or cotton balls, and Artificial Snow and Polytranspar Diamond Dust (both available from Wasco Wildlife Artists Supply, 800-334-8012). Wasco also markets a resin called Artificial Water that can be substituted for the EnviroTex used in this session.

Depending on the materials and techniques used, Jo can create raindrops, water puddles, freezing rain, ice, or snow—all sorts of foul weather conditions—which invite all manner of silly wild-foul art puns we won't get into.

Ice is created by dipping cotton into EnviroTex or Artificial Water, or by draping cotton along a tree branch and dribbling some of the liquid over it. Omit the cotton and you have water. Add Wasco's Artificial Snow to the epoxy and you have snow, which can be finished with a final application of Diamond Dust. The material dries to such a hard finish, says Jo, that you can scrub the surface with a soft brush and soapy water. Yet it looks very soft and fragile.

Jo notes that you should protect your carving, base, and other assorted habitat when working with these materials because the liquid tends to drip all over everything. Cover vulnerable areas with plastic wrap, foil, towels, or a similar protective covering.

Jo says she has found many items in the Wasco catalog that are applicable to bird carving. Wasco is mainly a taxidermy supplier, but many of their products are perfect for carvers, she says, "I highly recommend their Habitat and Exhibit Manual, which covers making snow, water, and plants and has an excellent section on the safe handling of chemicals."

The chief ingredient in creating water, ice, and snow is a clear plastic resin such as this two-part compound called EnviroTex Lite. Wasco's Artificial Water can be substituted.

When used alone, the plastic compound dries to a clear, high gloss and is perfect for creating droplets or puddles of water. Add some cotton, and the plastic becomes slightly opaque and frosty looking, like ice. Add a compound such as Artificial Snow (which appears to be finely ground Styrofoam), and you have powdery-looking dry snow. The plastic comes in two parts, and here Jo mixes parts A and B in a cup.

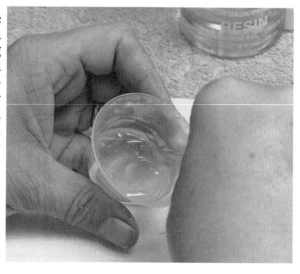

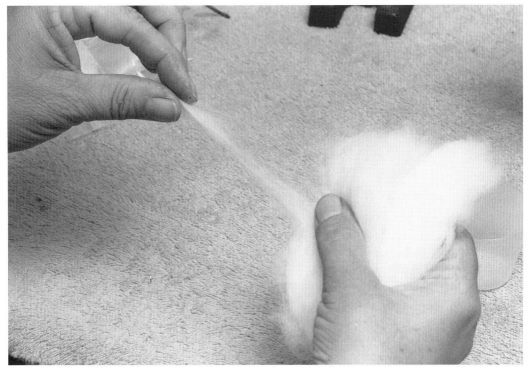

Jo pinches off a bit of cotton, preparing to create a
freezing rain look on a bare tree branch.

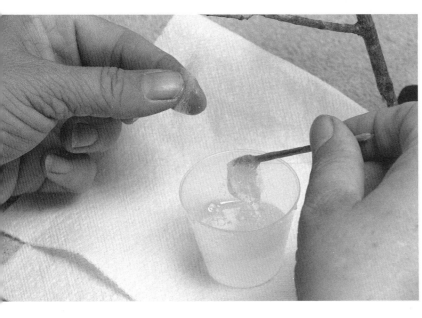

The cotton is dunked
into the plastic
compound and then is
strung along the
tree branch.

An alternative is to first drape the cotton along
the tree branch, then apply the plastic medium to
the cotton.

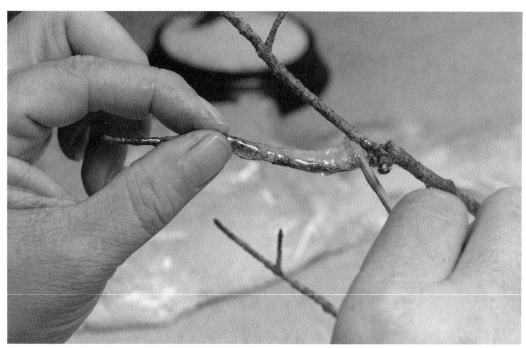

The cotton is saturated with plastic and is draped
along the limb, where Jo shapes it with tweezers
or wooden toothpicks. She will fluff the cotton
slightly with a pin to create a thawing snow look.

When the resin dries, it has a cloudy, icy look, thanks to the addition of the cotton.

A combination of resin and Artificial Snow produces a soft, crystalline appearance.

To cover a tree branch with snow, alternate applications of resin and Artificial Snow. Sprinkle a small amount of Diamond Dust on the finished snow while the resin is still tacky. It will produce a rock-hard surface that looks fragile but is long lasting and easy to clean.

9
Dirty Work

Jo Craemer

Creating realistic-looking rocks and dirt is not as easy as it sounds. You don't necessarily just go out to the garden, pick up a handful of humus, and add it to your carving. Usually the color and texture turn out wrong, especially if you're creating a habitat for a miniature carving. Ironically, the most realistic dirt and rocks are usually fakes.

Here is a technique Jo learned during a workshop with world champion carver Ernie Muehlmatt of Pennsylvania. All you need is a can of Durham Rock Hard Water Putty (available at hardware stores), an empty coffee can (or something similar), and some water.

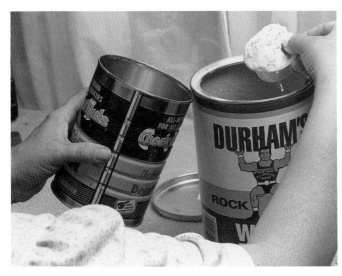

Jo begins by placing a few scoops of water putty into the coffee can.

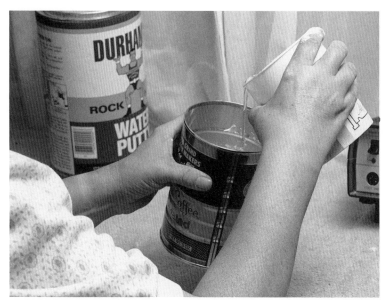

A little water is added, and the putty is stirred until it is smooth.

When the putty is mixed, Jo places the lid on the coffee can and shakes it vigorously.

You want a biscuit-dough consistency, Jo says, although this method of creating dirt and rocks is not an exact science. For different textures, vary the water/powder proportions.

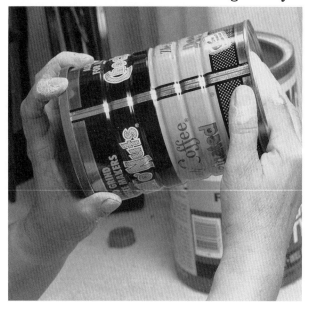

After about thirty seconds of shaking, the smooth mixture becomes an assortment of granules of different sizes and shapes.

Excess putty rocks can be saved and used in later habitat projects. Sort them according to size and store them in a glass jar or Ziploc bag.

Water putty was used to create the base for this carving of a quail. The sand-colored putty was used in its natural shade, but the material can be painted with acrylics either during mixing or after it dries. The paint soaks into the putty nicely, darkening the cracks and crevices.

Jo Craemer in her Georgetown, Delaware, studio. In addition to using water putty to create a rock and dirt habitat, she also recommends papier-mâché, which is mixed with water and dries to a rock-hard finish. She also uses a combination of Elmer's glue and sawdust, which creates an interesting medium to paint because the wood fibers will absorb washes of acrylic colors with varying concentrations, producing a polychromatic surface. Let the glue dry thoroughly before painting, she advises.

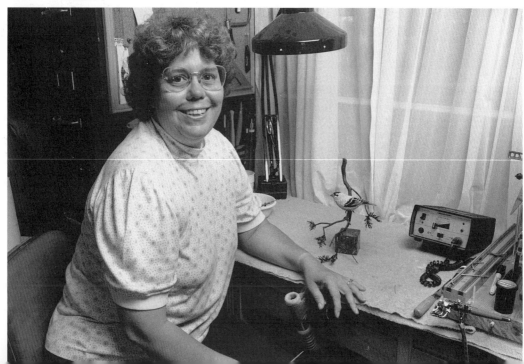

10 Larry Tawes, Jr.
Making Marsh Grass from Brass

Larry Tawes, Jr., grew up on the Chesapeake Bay on Maryland's Eastern Shore, fishing during the summer and dredging oysters aboard his family's skipjack during the winter. The bay has always been Larry's first form of recreation, and for many years it provided his livelihood. His first full-time job was as a mate on the sleek skipjack, one of the few working sailboats remaining on the bay.

It's not surprising, then, that as an artist, Larry's first choice of subject matter is waterfowl, and he often places the birds in habitat typical of the Chesapeake Bay region. In this session, Larry uses thin brass shim stock to make cordgrass similar to that growing along the Nanticoke River, his favorite waterfowl-hunting haunt.

Larry's technique is similar to that of Jo Craemer shown in chapter 4, but while Jo was making a bundle of attached blades suitable for a small songbird or a miniature carving, Larry's marsh reeds are on a much larger scale and incorporate rigid metal rods that function as support members as well as elements of habitat. When painted, the rods resemble stalks such as those found on cattail plants.

It's a fairly simple procedure. The thin metal is cut to resemble grass blades of various lengths, then a dull knife is used to score each blade. The blades are soldered together to form bunches, and then the grass is painted with acrylic colors applied with an airbrush. Although the procedure is straightforward, Larry adds his own refinements during the process, as the accompanying photos will show.

Larry still spends as much time as he can on the Chesapeake and its tributaries, but he no longer depends upon the bay's oysters for his living. At age thirty-three, he has been a full-time professional carver for more than ten years. He lives near the city of Salisbury and works in a backyard studio surrounded on two sides by a large aviary containing most species of North American waterfowl, as well as a few exotics.

Like many who have grown up along the shores of the Chesapeake, Larry developed an interest in waterfowl and decoy making at an early age. Larry's father, influenced by the work of Steve and Lem Ward of Crisfield, Maryland, began carving as a hobby in 1969, and it wasn't long before his son followed in his footsteps. "It was a typical father-son thing, I guess," Larry says. "He got interested in carving, and what he did, I wanted to do."

The Taweses began making hunting-style decoys and later switched to the more intricate decorative style. They found a growing market for their work, and by the late 1970s both were carving full-time.

Larry says he doesn't miss those freezing winter mornings on the skipjack, when they had to scatter hot coals over the deck to prevent ice from forming. His typical workday now begins and ends in his comfortable warm studio, where he sits in front of a large window looking out on the aviary.

The Chesapeake Bay is still an important resource for him, but now the bay serves a more creative function, providing inspiration and a sense of place for his wildfowl sculptures.

Larry begins by soldering together small brass rods that will serve as reeds, or stems. He uses rods of three sizes ($1/16''$, $1/8''$, and $3/16''$), which are available in most hobby shops or carving-supply businesses. The smaller rods slide into the next larger size, providing strength. Here Larry uses a propane torch to heat the joint between rods as he applies solder. Care must be taken to keep flammable materials away from the heat source, and Larry works in a well-ventilated area to avoid breathing fumes of melting solder.

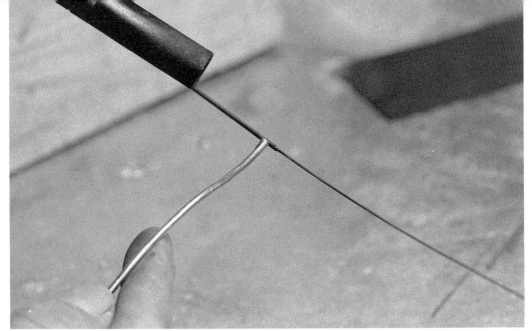

Larry will assemble brass stems of different lengths to use with the bundle of grass he is making. These rigid stems will help support the somewhat flimsy grass blades, which will be made from thin sheets of brass. The grass will be used with a full-size carving, so the assembled rods range from approximately 12 to 30 inches in length. The blades of grass will range in length from a few inches to perhaps 36 inches. The same techniques can be used when making habitat for miniature carvings.

When the solder has cooled and hardened, Larry uses a split mandrel on his Foredom tool and attaches a strip of 150-grit sandpaper. Because the reeds are made from brass tubes of three different sizes, it is important to grind down the solder joints, providing a smooth transition from one section to the next.

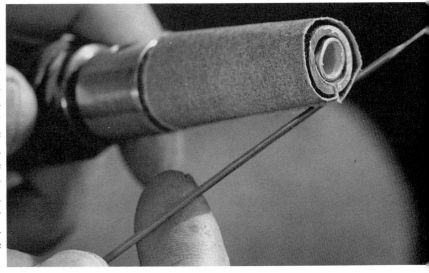

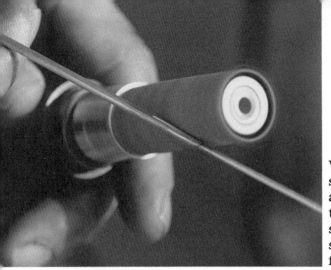

When ground down and painted, the solder joints will not be visible. Larry also uses the grinding tool to taper the ends of the reeds, creating a fairly sharp point on each. Larry grinds the solder joints in front of an exhaust fan to avoid breathing dust.

Larry will make the blades of cordgrass from brass shim stock, which is available in most hobby stores and carving-supply outlets. The brass Larry is using here is .005 inch thick. He begins by lightly sanding the metal to provide a good painting surface.

Stainless steel scissors are used to cut the brass sheets into random lengths of grass. Depending upon the size of the carving and its design, Larry may use only a few blades of grass or a bundle of a dozen or more individual blades.

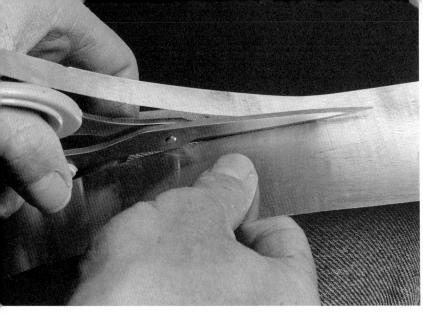

The brass blades are cut with a slight taper that comes to a point at the end of the blade. Larry warns that the thin pieces of brass are very sharp, so care should be taken.

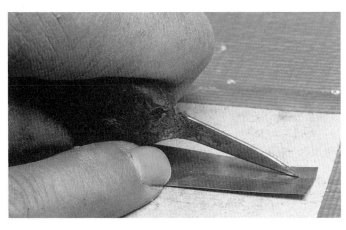

With the blades of grass cut out, Larry uses a dull number 8 Knott's knife to score each piece, drawing a series of lines down the length of the leaf.

It's important to use a dull blade because a sharp blade would pierce the thin metal. Score the metal on a soft, pliable base that will allow the brass to bend. Larry's base is a strip of vinyl flooring taped to his workbench.

A bundle of grass has been cut to random lengths and scored. Now Larry will solder together the individual blades and the brass stems he made earlier.

Each blade is scored two or three times. Scoring the metal gives it a lifelike look, replicating the rigid stems that run the length of a blade of cordgrass. Scoring also helps the metal stand upright by bending it slightly, creating an almost triangular shape.

Although the leaves of grass will stand on their own, they are not rigid enough to withstand much handling, so Larry uses the stronger metal rods as a foundation.

Larry begins with the taller stems, then adds the shorter ones, creating a composition with the taller blades in the center of the bundle. All the blades will bend slightly in the same direction, providing a windblown look.

He begins by soldering one of the longer leaves of grass to a brass rod, leaving approximately three-quarters of an inch of rod extending at the base. This will be used to mount the bundle of grass to a base.

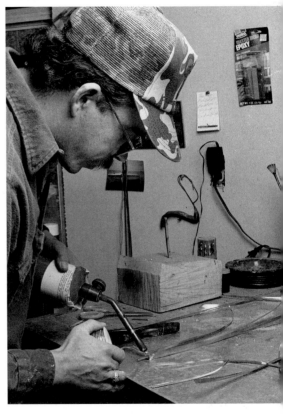

Once the bundle begins to take shape, it's tricky to add additional leaves without melting the solder on the leaves already in the group. Larry says the way to avoid this is to place a bead of solder on the leaf before adding it to the composition. He then applies just enough heat to cause the solder to melt when he adds the leaf to the group.

The second brass rod is added and more long leaves are soldered together.

Before going farther, Larry examines the composition of the bundle. Once the solder hardens, the leaves can be bent and shaped to any position desired.

More leaves are added, with the shorter blades on the outside of the composition.

It requires a balancing act to add the final few leaves without melting the solder that holds the group together. Larry places a bead of solder on each leaf, then adds it to the bundle, applying just enough heat to the back of the leaf to cause the solder to melt and adhere.

The bundle is now completed, the solder has hardened, and Larry makes a few final adjustments to the composition.

To add strength to the bundle, Larry carefully solders one of the flimsy taller leaves to the rigid brass stem.

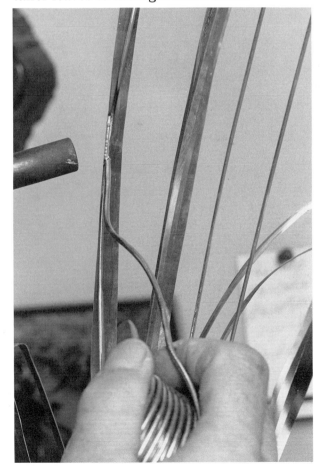

Before painting, Larry bends over a few of the blades of grass, providing a more natural look.

To provide a good painting surface, Larry uses his airbrush to apply a coat of lacquer to the metal. The hair dryer makes the lacquer set up quickly and prevents it from running. Larry dilutes the lacquer with 20 percent thinner before he applies it.

With the lacquer coat dry, Larry mixes acrylic paints, which also will be applied with the airbrush. Choice of color is purely subjective, depending upon the subject matter of the composition. Larry wants a winter look, so he will mix yellow oxide, raw umber, and warm white to come up with a dead-grass shade of tan. He uses Jo Sonya paints here, mixing equal parts of each and diluting them with water. Occasionally he will add a small amount of Liquitex yellow medium to the concoction to provide a more brilliant color.

He mixes the paints with water in a plastic film canister, shaking the canister until a uniform color is achieved.

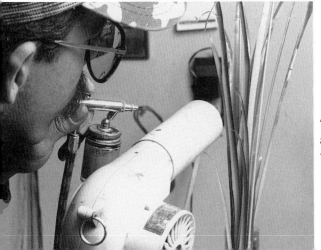

The paint is applied with the Badger airbrush, and the hair dryer is again used to speed up the drying process.

The final step calls for adding a few subtle imperfections; after all, marsh grass that has survived until January is likely to have all sorts of mold spots and discolorations. Larry adds these by dampening a toothbrush with well-diluted raw umber, then flicking the bristles with his thumb. The resultant random spray of dots is very realistic.

Care must be taken when handling the bundle during and after painting. The edges of the leaves are sharp, and if they scrape against each other they will remove paint. That's why Larry solders the longer leaves to the rigid brass rods. Be careful when using the hair dryer not to blow the leaves against each other.

Larry tries out his bundle of cord-grass next to a piece of driftwood by his pond. The ducks in the background seem to think it's realistic enough.

11

Rich Smoker
Carving a Monarch Caterpillar

Rich Smoker's career as a taxidermist prepared him well for his current profession as a bird carver, especially when it comes to creating habitat. As a taxidermist he made everything from realistic fall leaves to deer antlers. In this session Rich makes a bit of a departure from the usual habitat project in that he is creating replicas of living things to complement a bird carving, rather than the usual rocks, leaves, and other inanimate objects.

Rich began using two-part epoxy putty many years ago as a taxidermist, but as a wood sculptor he prefers to do as much work as possible in tupelo, including the various elements of habitat that are included in a presentation. Here he carves a very realistic monarch caterpillar from a piece of tupelo, then details it and paints it with acrylics.

The process is very much like carving a bird. Rich consults various reference material, sketches a caterpillar in the position he wants, then transfers the sketch to wood, drawing the top and side patterns onto a piece of tupelo. The pattern is cut out on a bandsaw, the form is rounded with a knife, and then detail is added with a high-speed grinder and an assortment of bits.

Once the carving is done, Rich seals the wood with lacquer, then paints it with acrylic paints, again using a field guide as reference.

Rich grew up in Selinsgrove, Pennsylvania, and developed an interest in bird carving while hunting ducks in local ponds and along the Susquehanna River. A need for hunting decoys led his father and him to carve a rig of black ducks, mallards, and canvasbacks while Rich was in high school, although his goal at that time was not a career in carving but in the related field of taxidermy.

After high school, Rich entered an apprenticeship in taxidermy and in 1979 opened his own business. Ironically, he began carving birds just as he was launching his taxidermy business, spending his slack season working with the carving tools.

"Other than that first hunting rig, I made my first decoys for a contest in 1979 and began my first decorative a year later," he says. "I realized I could carve decoys, but I couldn't carve them the way I wanted to, so I kept working at it. I knew the anatomy of the birds through taxidermy. I knew what they looked like from the inside out, but it was hard for me to take a piece of wood and make them look right from the outside in. I had no art education or background. I learned about mixing paints and using an airbrush in taxidermy training. When I finally discovered that carving had a lot in common with taxidermy as far as the sculptural aspects are concerned, I realized that carving wasn't as hard as I thought, and I began doing more of it and began to sell some."

Rich and his family moved to Crisfield, Maryland, in 1983 and he began to spend more time carving and less time doing taxidermy. In 1985 he quit taxidermy completely, except for preparing his own study skins.

Since the career move in 1979, Rich has won more than 230 ribbons in such competitions as the Ward World Championship in Ocean City, Maryland; the Mid-Atlantic in Virginia Beach, Virginia; the Havre de Grace and Chestertown shows in Maryland; the spring and fall shows in Chincoteague, Virginia; and numerous others. His decorative carvings and gunning decoys are in collections around the world.

Rich begins by studying field guides and photographs of caterpillars to come up with a shape and color that suits his particular project. He then makes a few sketches on paper, and when he is satisfied with the design, he transfers the outline to a piece of tupelo. Here he sketches the top/bottom outline of the monarch caterpillar.

As the side view is drawn, Rich sketches the feet, antennae, and body segments, just to get an idea of the proportions of the caterpillar. These lines will be removed during the carving process. The roughing-out procedure used here—sketching and cutting out side and top/bottom views—is the same method Rich uses in making decoys.

The outline is cut out on the bandsaw, then the top of the caterpillar is rounded with a carving knife. The bottom will be left squared off for now, and in later steps Rich will carve individual feet. A center line has been drawn along the top and bottom.

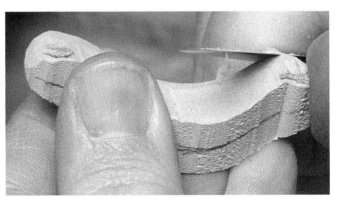

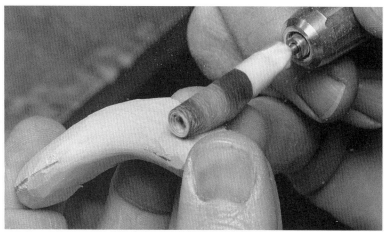

With the top rounded, Rich uses a split mandrel and medium-grit sandpaper in his high-speed grinder to smooth the surface of the wood and remove knife marks.

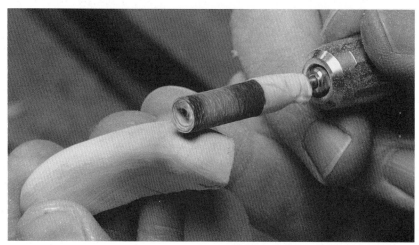

At the rear of the caterpillar is a single large foot. Rich uses the sander to taper the body slightly at the foot.

Before carving the individual feet and the body segments, Rich uses a stone bit on his grinder to bevel the bottom edges of the caterpillar.

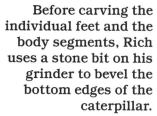

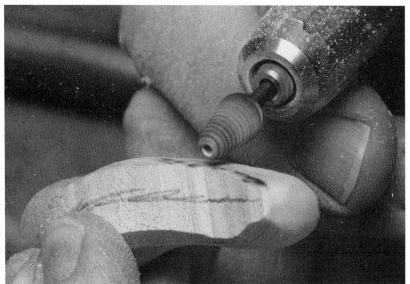

The stone creates a slight angle where the feet will be carved. The caterpillar's feet bend under its body somewhat, so beveling the bottom edge before carving the feet makes the job easier.

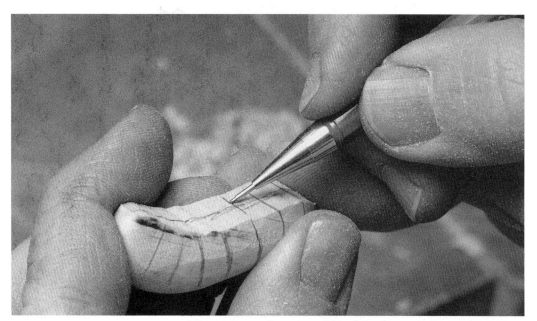

The monarch caterpillar has ten or eleven large, well-defined body segments, and Rich uses a pencil to sketch these along the bottom and lower sides. Each body segment has two small feet. Rich will first carve the feet, then the segments on the upper body.

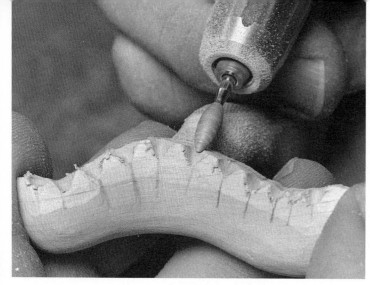

He uses a rounded bit on his high-speed grinder to define each foot, using the pencil lines as a guide.

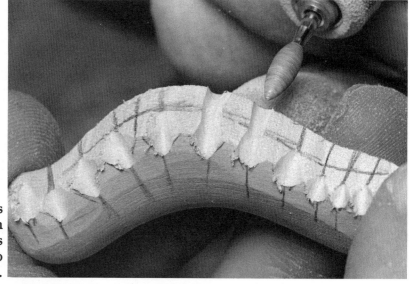

Rich carves grooves on each side, then uses the grinder to connect them.

The same bit is used to remove wood along the length of the caterpillar's body. When this step is completed, the feet will be well defined.

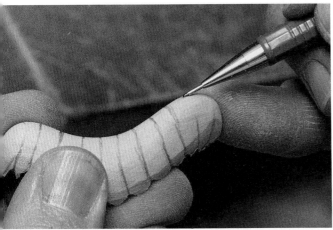

Now Rich is ready to carve the body segments. He extends the pencil lines around the body of the caterpillar, using the location of the feet as a guide. The feet should be at the centers of each segment.

A small, cylindrical ruby stone is used to relieve the segments following the pencil lines. The segments are smaller and closer together at the ends of the caterpillar.

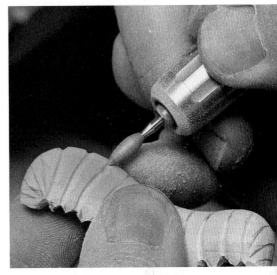

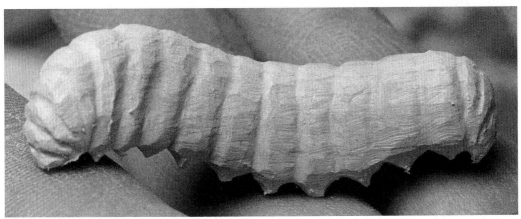

With the segments roughed out, the monarch looks like this.

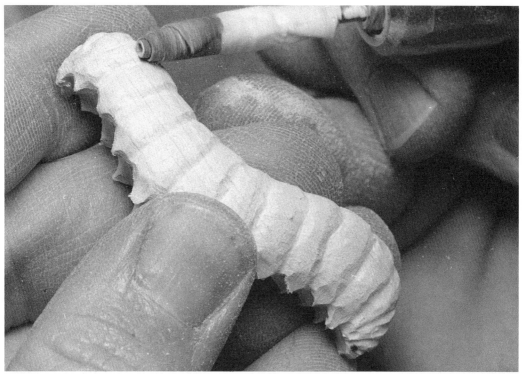

Rich again sands the caterpillar, using fine paper
in his split mandrel. Sanding removes the lines left
by the carving tool, making the segments more
subtle.

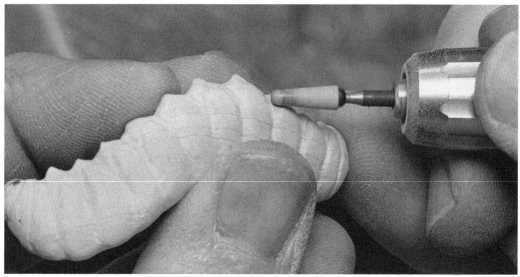

A fine stone cutter is used on the grinder to further define each segment, smoothing the contours.

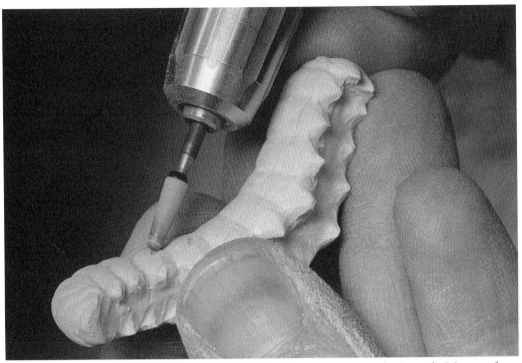

The same bit is used to carve little wrinkles and
dimples that appear above the feet.

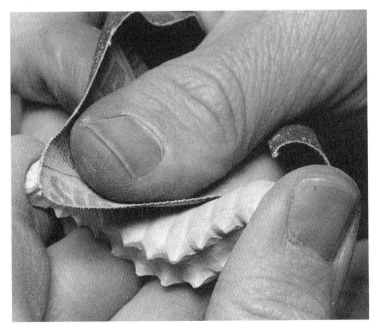

The caterpillar is
again sanded lightly,
this time by hand.

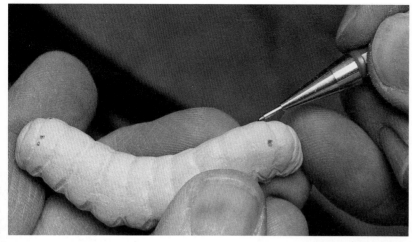

Now Rich is ready to insert the antennae. The monarch has two on each end; the pair at the head are slightly longer. He begins by using a pencil to mark where holes will be drilled to accommodate the antennae.

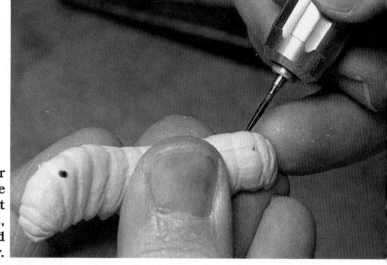

A small bit on the grinder is used to drill the holes. The antenna should be bent at an angle of about 45 degrees, so the holes are drilled accordingly.

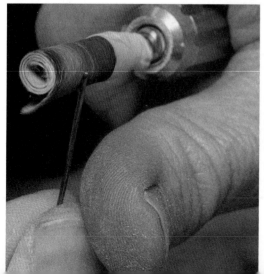

The antennae are made of thin wire. Here Rich is using the leftover stems cut from glass eyes; and flexible wire of the appropriate diameter will do. The wire should be sanded to a gradual taper.

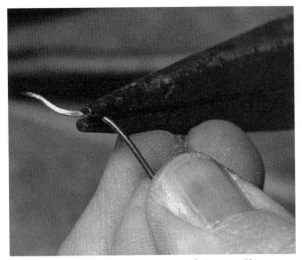

The wire is bent to shape with needle-nose pliers, then cut off and inserted into the drilled holes. Two-part epoxy is used to cement the wire in the holes.

Rich makes a few adjustments to the angle of the wire before the epoxy cures.

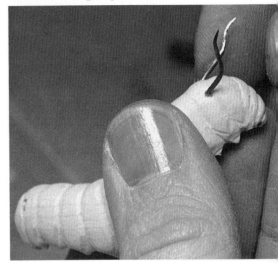

With the body carved and the antennae inserted, the caterpillar is ready for painting.

Rich uses field guides and photographs from nature magazines to determine the correct color. The caterpillar is only about two inches long, so he inserts a small screw in the bottom to serve as a handle during painting. A hole should be drilled to accommodate the screw to avoid splitting the wood.

Rich sprays the carving with lacquer thinner to seal the wood, then applies several coats of white gesso to provide a uniform painting surface. Gesso is applied to the metal antennae as well as the wooden body.

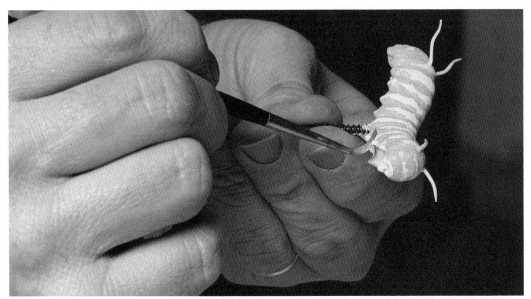

Rich begins with a coat of titanium white acrylic paint, then paints stripes using three different shades of yellow. First he applies wide stripes with cadmium yellow light, then darkens the edges of the stripes with yellow medium and yellow-orange.

Rich uses carbon black to paint black stripes, the feet, and the antennae.

He finishes the painting by touching up the stripes with titanium white, making the white areas wider.

A couple of coats of matte medium and varnish
give the painted monarch a waxy, lifelike look.

Rich uses two-part epoxy cement to mount the
caterpillar on a wooden stem.

12
Making an Epoxy Snake

Rich Smoker

In this brief demonstration, Rich shows how to make a realistic snake using two-part epoxy putty. Rich worked with epoxy for many years in the taxidermy business, and in this session he combines his skill at working with epoxy with his ability to carve and paint.

A bead of epoxy is rolled out and coaxed into the proper position. When it hardens, Rich shapes the head, eyes, and other detail with a grinder, then paints it with acrylics.

Putty is handy for making snakes because it is flexible and can be draped in a variety of positions. It is available in hardware and plumbing-supply stores as well as from carving- and taxidermy-supply houses.

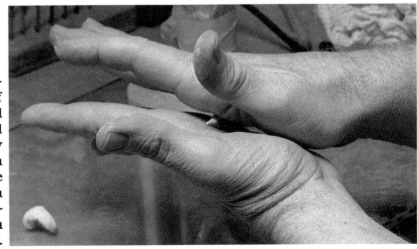

Rich begins by mixing the two parts of the epoxy well and then molding a small string approximately one-eighth inch in diameter. This snake will be used with a miniature bird carving, so it will be much smaller than lifesize.

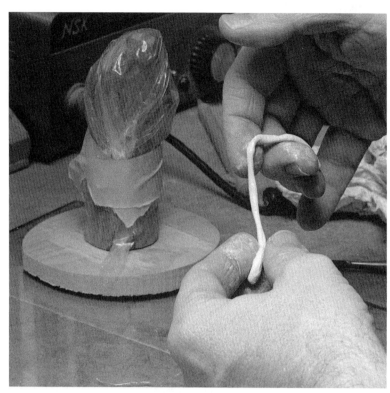

The wooden branch on which the snake will be mounted is covered with thin plastic, and the snake is rolled out to its approximate shape and length.

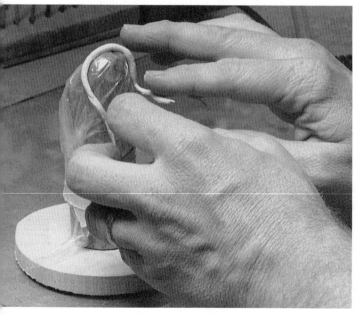

The snake is draped along the covered branch as Rich tries various shapes and postures. The plastic allows the snake to be molded to the proper shape without actually adhering to the wooden surface. When the epoxy hardens, it will be removed from the mount, carved and painted, and then returned to its permanent position.

Rich uses dental tools to add some detail to the pliable epoxy.

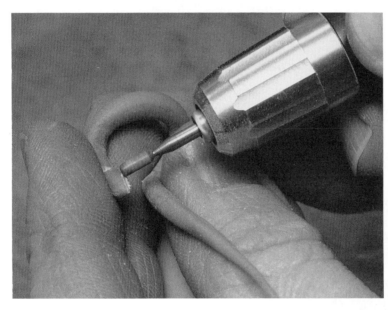

Most of the detail is added with the grinder after the epoxy has hardened. Here Rich shapes the head with a small ruby cutter mounted on a high-speed grinder.

This will be a garter snake, and Rich begins painting by applying a coat of mars black acrylic to the entire snake.

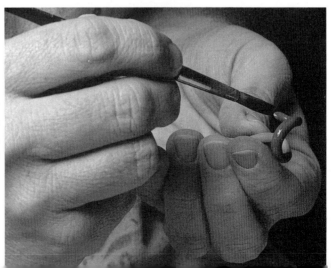

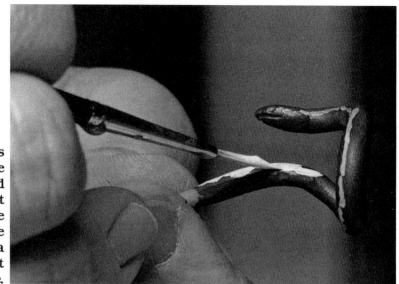

A size 1 brush is used to paint the belly white, tinted slightly with a bit of raw umber. The stripe on the side is painted with a mix of yellow light and white.

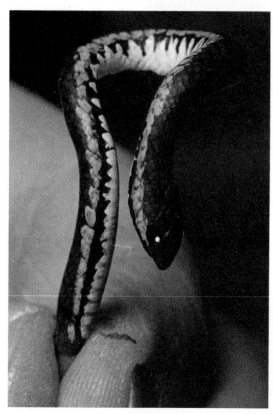

Rich then applies additional black detail over the white and yellow. A field guide is used as reference during painting. Careful application of black duplicates the look of scales, as seen here. The snake will later be used with a bird carving, possibly as the prey of a hawk or wading bird.

About the Author

Curtis Badger has written widely about wildfowl art, wildfowl hunting, and conservation issues in general. His articles have appeared in many national and regional magazines, and he serves as editor of *Wildfowl Art Journal*, which is published by the Ward Foundation. He is the coauthor of *Painting Waterfowl with J. D. Sprankle, Making Decoys the Century-Old Way*, and *Barrier Islands*. He lives in Onley, Virginia, and is currently working on a book about salt marsh ecology.

Other Books of Interest to Bird Carvers

How to Carve Wildfowl
The masterful techniques of nine international blue-ribbon winners.
by Roger Schroeder

How to Carve Wildfowl Book 2
Features eight more master carvers and the tools, paints, woods, and techniques they use for their best-in-show carvings.
by Roger Schroeder

Waterfowl Carving with J. D. Sprankle
A fully illustrated reference to carving and painting 25 decorative ducks.
by Roger Schroeder and James D. Sprankle

Painting Waterfowl with J. D. Sprankle
Over 400 spectacular color photos illustrate this incomparable painting guide. Includes step-by-step instruction for 13 projects and color charts for exact paint mixes.
by Curtis J. Badger and James D. Sprankle

Making Decoys the Century-Old Way
Detailed, step-by-step instructions on hand-making the simple yet functional working decoys of yesteryear.
by Grayson Chesser and Curtis J. Badger

Decorative Decoy Designs
Bruce Burk's three volumes (*Dabbling and Whistling Ducks, Diving Ducks,* and *Geese and Swans*) are complete guides to decoy painting by a renowned master of the art. All three feature life-size color patterns, reference photographs, alternate position patterns, and detailed paint-mixing instructions.
by Bruce Burk

John Scheeler, Bird Carver
A tribute to the bird-carving world's master of masters, John Scheeler.
by Roger Schroeder

Carving Miniature Wildfowl with Robert Guge
Scale drawings, step-by-step photographs and painting keys demonstrate the techniques that make Guge's miniatures the best in the world.
by Roger Schroeder and Robert Guge

Songbird Carving with Ernest Muehlmatt
Muehlmatt shares his expertise on painting, washes, feather flicking, and burning, plus insights on composition, design, proportion, and balance.
by Roger Schroeder and Ernest Muehlmatt

For complete ordering information, write:
Stackpole Books
P.O. Box 1831
Harrisburg, PA 17105
or call 1-800-READ-NOW